Mario Mantese

Prayers from the Divine Source

AF188939

Mario Mantese

Prayers
*from the
Divine Source*

Translated from the German by Mark Albin

Typesetting and Cover design by Marion Musenbichler
Cover illustration © fotolia.com/muama, Tierney
Illustration inside © fotolia.com/Eva105

Original Title: Gebete aus der heiligen Quelle
© 2009 first published by Drei Eichen Verlag,
D-97762 Hammelburg

ISBN: 978-3-7481-9189-6

© 2019 by Mario Mantese
www.mariomantese.com

First Edition in English
Printing and Production by BoD – Books on Demand, Norderstedt

$\mathcal{D}$ear Reader,

When you pray, you call to the Divine. You pray to what you discover within yourself, to *the Heavenly Kingdom,* to the spark of that which radiates its supreme brilliance through everything, the *Light of all Lights.* Master Jesus spoke of it in this way: *It is the kingdom of God within you.*

I have written these prayers for you and they flow out of my heart. Now, with great intensity and brightness, they flow into yours.

These prayers are most potent when you read them aloud. After each prayer, close your eyes and allow the words to work within you in silence!

May these pearls of light gift you with immeasurable strength, love, confidence, and deep healing!

$\mathcal{MM}$

*L*ight of All Lights,
oh, thriving force,
You glow
deep within my heart.
Your immeasurable abundance
flows through me
by day and by night.
Before I even think of You,
You are already here,
You, the radiant ordering power
in my life.
Speechless and astonished,
my heart dedicates itself to you.
Every fiber of my earthly being
bathes in Your splendor.

$\mathcal{D}$ivine flow of grace,
Without You there would be nothing
of that which is,
for everything that is, is You.
You, all-protecting, all-penetrating grace,
unfathomable is your luminous,
limitless abundance.
Boundless grace grants me strength
to leave all illusions behind,
and thus to experience
the immense beauty of the unlimited
Divine within me.
Grace grants me strength
to shake off and overcome old habits.
Yes, without doubt, without hesitation,
I turn to You now:
grace, this subtle, luminous current
within me.

My heart does not belong to me;
my life does not belong to me.
My heart and my life
belong to You, God.
Nothing belongs to me.
Everything belongs to God,
for God is everything that is.
You, Dear God, never withhold anything,
and never turn me away.
What amazing fortune, what a blessing!
God sees me,
because I see him.
He calls me,
because I call him.

4

I no longer focus,
on my wayfaring thoughts,
and discover through this letting go
gentle devotion.
Devotion transcends my thoughts,
and erases my dreamy ignorance.
Tranquility settles within.
Volatile, destructive ideas
no longer tie or trouble me,
for devotion *unties* me,
and love *unites* me.
Love is pure grace.
My heart is filled
with the gentle love,
which flows from You, God.

5

*T*he vast riches
which are inherent to love,
testify to the illumination
and the magnificence
which You are, God.
Within this force of love
and through this force of love,
the entire cosmos emerges.
Through this divine force of love
and within it,
the entire cosmos dissolves once again.
What majestic power abides
in the certitude that I am One
with this unwavering universal love,
with these incalculable riches.

The celestial fire burns
with immense grandeur within me.
The divine stream of light
flows through me
with unlimited power.
What an unfathomable mystery!
A current in which
the entire universe flows;
which *is* the entire universe;
a current without beginning
and without end.
How supreme the confidence,
that I do not flow separately
from this divine current,
and that this current is
my boundless life within You, God.

My silent soul perceives
the glorious radiance of God,
and dissolves in this grace.
I now distance myself
from gloomy, unnecessary thoughts,
that the blessing can touch me,
and completely transform me.
I flow out of darkness
and back into the light,
and see this clearly now:
"One who loves You, God,
is one You love."

8

$\mathscr{T}$he power of the soul
can open inner doors.
In the treasure storehouse of light,
heavenly endowments are available
in abundance.
They reveal themselves within me,
as soon as I release myself
from the order of human beings,
and align myself with the cosmic order.
Here, I experience that both orders
are Your *one* order.
The power of soul is not the force of will.
The power of soul is supra-personal,
unconditional love.
I align myself with this unconditional love,
knowing that all will be good.
I do not hesitate and do not doubt,
and have deep faith,
for the kingdom of light
already resides within me.

I am not lost in the throws of death
simply because I am rooted in the flesh.
The realm of life where time passes
is merely my temporary home.
My true home is at the primal source
of the Light of All Lights.
I do not hesitate and do not doubt,
for now I know
that everything is in God,
and You, God, are in me.
Surges of joy flow through
each cell of my body.
A heavenly transformation takes place.
Divine powers flow
like golden rays into my heart,
and wake it from its thousand-year sleep.
The supreme heavenly force fills me,
bestowing me
with clarity and transparence.

My soul becomes powerful,
sanctified and adorned,
for I have now shifted my gaze
away from the ephemeral.
I never look back
into the past,
and now cross over
the shore of the transient world.
Yes, I now enter
my divine home.
It is within me.

Through blessings pervaded with light,
from pure love overflowing,
I emerge from the ancient mist.
I do not hesitate and do not doubt,
for this one first small step
leads me up the high mountain.
The first step is most important,
that I move internally,
and this I do *now*.
You, the great gardener,
are removing the old heavy stones
from my heart,
and moistening my soul
with heavenly waters.

Oh, how magnificent!
In the vital Here and Now,
there is no abyss
and no suffering.
With gentle eyes,
I turn my gaze inwards,
and see my true presence.
I do not look back anymore,
for there is nothing there
for me to see –
only physical, fleeting trifles.
I no longer think back,
for there is nothing there
for me to think about –
only what has already been thought.
My heart abides in You, God.

The nourishing force of Nature
is sacred,
my body is sacred,
all living beings are sacred,
all water is sacred,
all trees are sacred,
all plants are sacred,
the Earth is sacred,
my true presence is sacred.
I observe the world
with eyes of love,
for the world is
the sacred robe of God,
and You, God,
live within me.

To make mistakes is human.
To see a mistake as a mistake is human.
To admit a mistake is a mistake is human.
Not to repeat mistakes is human.
There are no mistake-free human beings,
but yes, there are those who lack insight.
From now on, I belong to those
with insight and sincerity,
and I am ready at all times to forgive.
That is human.
The power of insight and forgiveness
is indeed divine and human.
To forgive a little bit is nothing,
to forgive *totally* is *everything* –
I see this clearly.
Oh, what glorious, grace-filled power
abides in forgiveness.
I do not hesitate and do not doubt.
I am ready *now* to truly forgive.

The fine fragrance of forgiveness
brings peace, and peace is truly divine.
Never again will I shun an opportunity
to forgive, for missed opportunities
never come again.
I forgive myself and forgive my fellow
humans – this is the path to true peace.
In forgiveness and in peace,
I recognize how incredibly precious
my own essential being is.
This divine radiance
has never wandered from me,
though my eyes have certainly wandered,
and my field of vision was blurred.
Therefore, I now direct my gaze
away from darkness and into the light,
and penetrate though all the mind's mist.
I do not hesitate and do not doubt,
and free myself from everything
that weakens me.

16

*B*enevolent and purifying
are the virtues of Your heavenly powers.
I trust in them, for they are closer to me
than my hand or foot.
There is not one moment,
when the connection
to Your divine powers,
to union with You would be severed,
for these brilliant wonders
are dormant within my heart.
I now grant them
the opportunity to awaken.
A deep look at my impermanent life
on the Earth is truly a wonderful means
of waking up.
Humble reverence deepens the affinity
to those divine regulating forces,
which guide me to the unalterable One,
and bring me home.

*M*y soul submerges
in the radiant luster of eternal abundance,
in this shoreless ocean of light.
This majesty transcends my intellect.
This grace cannot be grasped
with human language.
You, oh immeasurable light
which encompasses everything
and embraces everything,
erase all shadows
and all ambiguity within me.
Deep gratitude fills my heart.

The unalterable majesty of God
is like a gentle smile –
a smile
that removes all my worries.
You, eternal God,
smile into my heart,
and my heart smiles back.

After aligning my heart
with the sunlit truth,
an emerging beauty
awakens in my heart.
This superb power transforms me,
and creates me anew.
The old ego-pain melts here,
and the old ways vanish.
I do not hesitate and do not doubt,
and accept this glorious emergence
completely, and assimilate it
completely into my being.
Within it I discover
that which eternally gives,
and I experience how it changes me.
Yes, I myself become
that which eternally gives.
What unfathomable grace!

Hesitating no more,
doubting no more
I now, through the grace of God,
overcome the coercing forces of death
within me.
Your realm of light manifests sooner
than the blink of an eye;
the realm of light is
within me.
Where your light shines,
all shadows fade away.
Inside myself, I see them vanish.

*S*elf-pity is another word
for depression.
Giving up is another expression
for resignation.
I do not resign myself;
I stand up now,
and devote attention
to the immense energy of the heavens
which lies dormant within me.
It waits to be awakened.
This heavenly energy
eliminates all worries;
I can already see this clearly.
I no longer worry about my worries,
and allow You, the Light of All Lights,
to guide my life.
Without doubt, without procrastination,
I shake off everything that weakens me.

Your heavenly power helps me
to emancipate myself
from the web of suffering.
Never again will I remain dull and passive,
so I may encounter Your divine light.
Without hesitation and without doubt,
I approach the heavenly light,
and travel upon its rays
into the internal sun.
Because I do not turn away,
the divine waters of life
permeate my being.
All floodgates are wide open.

*N*ow I see the splendor
and gentle beauty of my life.
I ascend,
refreshed and full of energy,
from the grave
of all negative thoughts.
In this way
I experience a deep transformation.
Hesitating no more,
doubting no more,
I set my sights
on the immeasurable glory
which already resides
within me.

I look deeply within myself,
and now I understand:
it is never wrong to ask for help.
But true help awakens
from self-surrender.
Indeed, help always arrives,
but usually in a different way
than one thinks or expects.
Because I now entrust my life to you, God,
I know that help is already there
before I ask for it.
Your healing, liberating support
flows into me endlessly.
Oh, how wonderful; I need not desire
or seek the help of the Divine.
It is always – here and now – within me,
when I align myself
with the Light of All Lights.

The journey through the shadows
does not take long,
when, without hesitation and free of doubt,
I turn to pure love.
Love never speaks to my earthly 'I'.
Love speaks to my intuitive intelligence.
I cannot chase after pure love,
cannot covet it or wish for it.
Otherwise, I seal it away in my heart
and disturb its wondrous flow.
The glow of pure love was already there
before I was born.
It will also be here after I have left
my physical body behind.
To live consciously
within love's illumination *now*,
is uplifting and transforming.

*S*eeing through the delusions,
seeing to the bottom of the old stories
has truly 'dis-illusioned' me.
No longer hesitating,
no longer doubting,
I extricate myself from everything
that burdens my heart.
The journey through these delusions
ends here and now.

Yes, I am ready *now*,
to say farewell forever
to all the bitter experiences
I have known.
The dark traces recorded in my memory
I pass on to You,
the Light of All Lights.
Within you, all shadows vanish.

What can I do?
I stop lying to myself,
stop deceiving myself,
and stop feeling sorry for myself.
I have absolute faith
in Your divine light,
which resides within me,
the source of all energy, You.
When I help myself,
God helps me.

I stop making my life
unnecessarily complicated,
and discover the Universal
in its absolute simplicity
within me.
No longer will I contend and quarrel
with my own life,
for my true presence
is truly precious and divine,
and what is divine
abides in You, oh God.

The long night ends here and now.
I sense the flow of heavenly light
within me.
I do not hesitate, and accept
this magnificent gift unconditionally,
for what is offered in this way
comes forth from You, God.
Resolute, I take hold
of Your redeeming hand,
which pulls me out of the mire of mortality.
Yes, I am ready *now*,
and shed my heavy, century-old,
worn-out earthly overcoat,
and elevate myself
beyond past and future.
The lightness of being within You, God,
returns to my innermost heart.
Fears and doubts depart
like shadows under the sun.
What incredible grace!

The gateway into the realm of light
is completely open,
but the passage is narrow.
My doubts and my procrastinating
have created
these narrowing constraints.
Because I now completely turn
to the divine light,
all obstructions
and everything narrow within me
dissolves,
and I become aware
of my boundless being
within You,
Light of All Lights.

*T*omorrow,
today will already be the past.
I see now
that other than *Here and Now*,
there is nothing,
and that this *Here and Now*
carries your name, God.
The *'pure land'* is here and now.
Therefore it is not possible,
that I live separate or outside
of this *'pure land'*.
It is within me,
and flows through me.
What magnificent grace!

31

*T*he place I am *now,*
is the place where I *always was*.
It carries the name *God*.
This heavenly place
which I longed to find,
where I yearned to go
is already manifest within me.
I suffered harm
when, through negligence,
I distanced myself
from this heavenly place,
from You, God.
Now, I am attentive,
and see exactly where I go,
and where I live.

I awaken in the potent radiance
of God,
I awaken in universal love.
Now I recognize my noble heritage
in You, oh God.
The power of death was only a dream,
from which I now finally awaken.
I discover immeasurable beauty
and immeasurable divine power
within me.
What grace!
Worries and fears
have no more power over me,
for I have ceased
to nourish and vitalize them
with the energy of thought.
Unburdened and unbound,
I return back to the lightness of my being.
Never again will I depart
from this boundless expanse within.

My earthly form seeks renewal,
seeks transformation.
Heavenly power embraces me,
heavenly power calls to me,
and brings me home.
The luminous wave
that touches my heart
is this divine voice
which calls to me.
I listen to it,
and without hesitating,
without doubting,
I accept it.

When I wanted to follow
an inner path,
I encountered hindrances
and never arrived at my goal.
The path was never the goal.
The glory of God pervades me now,
for I have completely let go
of ideas of a path and a goal.
I do not attain satisfaction
through my actions;
I find it only
in the silence
of my heart.

Amidst the world of death,
You, heavenly light,
shine in my heart.
Finally, I can distinguish You
and accept You.
I have doubted and hesitated too long.
Obstacles have obstructed my view
and covered my heart in shadows.
But now, I raise my gaze
beyond all obstacles,
and allow the spirit of love,
the spirit of liberation,
to touch, awaken, and guide
my heart.

The bonds of sorrow and fear
plunge my heart into darkness.
However menacing
the darkness may appear,
rays of divine light are always close by,
and shine through into every small crack
in my soul.
I open wide my heart,
and allow the divine light to enter.
Sorrow and fear melt away.
My deepest gratitude.

Where there is a spring,
living beings come to drink.
I thirst
and drink to my heart's content.
The spring remains continually
full to the brim,
for truly,
the heavenly waters
are available in abundance.
These vitalizing waters
are granted to all.
They now flood my heart.
I drink
as much as I possibly can.

38

I immerse myself in the silence,
in the boundless tenderness
of my soul.
This flow of grace,
without beginning and without end,
is the source of all splendor.
I submerge and drown
in the divine ocean,
in eternal Here and Now.
My heart is free of wanting or coveting,
and without conflict.
Universal love flows into me,
and flows out through me.
Nothing happens tomorrow.
Everything is now.
I am now.

To become active myself
is the best help for my life.
When I sincerely examine my weaknesses,
corrections in my life are possible.
What is the use of asking You, God,
to act for me,
when I remain passive and dull?

Yes, *now* I am ready for the great renewal,
and take my life responsibly
into my own hands.
Because I do not hesitate, do not wait,
and do not doubt,
Your divine help is assured.
I vigorously break through
my inner darkness,
and recognize the immeasurable
grandeur of my being.

I recognize the power
which resides in devotion,
and trust in
the Light of All Lights.
All indolence, all doubts,
and all procrastination
I leave behind me –
If not now, then when?

I think in one direction,
look in another direction,
and live in another direction.
My customs and habits
were created this way.
I accustomed myself to those around me,
and hoped that those around me
would also become accustomed to me.
But customs and habits
make me rigid and dull –
I see this *now*.

Therefore, I begin
gently to de-accustom myself.
De-accustomed, it is possible for me
to be vital and open
living together with other living beings,
without merely accustoming myself
to someone or something.

The more I de-accustom myself
from the singular and the particular
the more comprehensively You, God,
live in me.
But to de-accustom does not mean
to separate oneself from another person.
It means sharing and togetherness
in freedom from stagnating habits.

I prevail over each and every form
of negativity within me,
over each and every negative attitude
towards life.
Never again will I think: "I cannot".
Otherwise, I plunge
into old harmful mind-states
that weaken me.
I remain vigilant.
I remain vital.
This is easy for me now,
for I know that You, God,
are truly close by
and guiding me.

I take in deeply
the immeasurable love
which resides within me.
This unalterable love
is my home –
I see this clearly now.
I have never left it,
and it has never left me.
I am always here and now,
and *it* is always here and now.
The love of the heavens
flows within my heart,
and my heart abides in You, God.
This is how I live *now*,
in harmonious accordance
with the love of the heavens,
and that is good.

43

One who loves God,
is one God loves.
I do not hesitate and do not doubt,
and dedicate myself completely
to the Light of All Lights.
The shadows of death
can no longer touch me,
for my home is within You,
the Light of All Lights.

Silently, I bathe in divine light,
in the ocean of fulfillment and joy.
Now I am mindful,
and allow my thoughts
no more opportunity
to create separation within me.
I no longer let them wander aimlessly
in yesterday and tomorrow.

I live here and now,
embedded in universal love,
immersed in joy and contentment
without cause.
Never again
will joy and contentment
stray from my innermost being,
because I am wide awake and mindful
now.

The old borders have disappeared;
my strenuous wanderings are over.
The old dream has been erased.
Oh, how magnificent,
to finally be home again!
I breathe and live within You,
Light of All Lights,
and am awe-struck and amazed
at the boundless divine love
which shows itself to me.
My soul abides in peace.

I do not hesitate;
I enter the Light of All Lights.
I will lack nothing.
In You, Light of All Lights,
all my fears and worries
are cleared away.
When I was wandering
in the valley of deathly shadows,
You were always with me.
All my doubts fade and vanish,
for You, oh eternal light,
have entered my heart.
Through You I experience
transformation and resurrection.
You rejuvenate my soul,
and bestow me with eternal life.

I thought
I was here and you there, oh God,
until you dissolved
the continent of borders within me.
Now I walk
in your grace
and breathe in your splendor.
The blind pushing forward
that was my everyday life
is over.
I am home at last,
in silence.

I drink water
from a hidden source,
which grants eternal life.
Floods sent from the heavens
have washed away the old world
and divulged to me
unlimited wealth and fulfillment.
The earthly night
has given way
to the brilliant sacred red of dawn.
The old images have vanished forever.
I am eternally here and now
in the brilliant abundance
of God.

Because I have let you, Dear God,
into my heart,
You have, through Your grace,
opened wide for me the gateway
to the ocean of wisdom.
My intellect would never
have been capable
of entering this ocean of wisdom –
I see this clearly now.
My thinking and my desire
to understand
were defeated at the frontier
of my knowledge.
Yes, God cannot be a thought,
or an object of analysis or understanding.
Only deep, unwavering love for You,
the most divine of all
within my heart,
is the key that can open
the gateway to the ocean of wisdom.

*M*y self-seeking
and my old egotism
pose challenges –
this I truly see.
And just because of this,
from now on
I am wide awake,
that I see through
these deceptive, egocentric energies,
and what they do.
Because my heart is now
completely dedicated to You,
this penetrating and overcoming
is easy and effortless.

50

*T*he greatest joy floods my heart,
because my consciousness begins
to gently let go
of my countless dark thoughts.
I flow back into the most sacred of all,
and accept patiently what occurs:
a great purification and refinement.
I do not hesitate or doubt.
I trust completely.

The gravity of my old dull life
in the physical body
pulls me down
and separates me from God.
This is terribly painful,
and causes me suffering.
Therefore, I turn my gaze
to my luminous spiritual home,
and see,
– thanks to You, God –
no border anywhere.
Nothing stops me
from dedicating myself now
completely to You,
the Light of All Lights.

The soft radiance of God
is the power that flows
through everything in the cosmos.
It allows my old willpower to melt,
and leads me into
a never-ending, luminous expanse.
I now flow silently
with this divine current
that has no beginning and no end,
and merge with this heavenly force.
My heart breaks open;
I let it.
Your divine current
carries me through life,
and shapes it anew.
I let it.

53

*M*y light-filled heart
abides in deep silence,
because it has entered
the divine current.
Like a thousand golden radiating suns,
the great mystery is unveiled –
the Unimaginable, the Inconceivable.
Healing and blessing
glow within me, through me.
Healing and blessing
transform me.
I flow back gently
into the ocean of wisdom.

*S*ometimes I am unhappy.
I don't feel well,
and I suffer.
It happens.
But now,
I no longer let myself be chained
to my physical body
and to the world.
for the body and the world do not suffer;
I suffer.

I raise myself up
and go within,
towards the source of heavenly energy.
To live in suffering
certainly cannot be
the purpose of my life.
Therefore, I dedicate myself now
to You, God, the great purpose.

I do not complain,
and have no self-pity.
Energetic and resolute,
I leave the old pains inside me behind.
I ascend to the divine source,
flow out of the darkness,
and into the light.
My original home
is always here and now –
is this divine source.

*N*ow, I listen to that
which is behind my 'I',
to that which is behind my thinking.
I now become aware
of my universal vitality
within You, God,
and see how the black veil of my 'I'
slowly dissolves.
Heavenly light flows into the center.
The shadow-like forms
on the outer periphery
do not really exist.
The light in the center
is my true home.
I give the land of shadows
no more attention.

56

*E*goism leads me along false pathways.
Egoistic behavior weakens me.
With courage,
I look meticulously
at my previous habits of behavior,
and resolutely stop repeating them,
now.
What happens then?
After that, the walls of the old dam
crash down,
and the divine water
flows freely everywhere.
Never again
will I feed and sustain old stories
with the power of my thinking.
Ceasing to do this
brings liberation.

I no longer allow unimportant things
a place in my life.
My life is too precious.
How many precious days on the Earth
have I squandered with banal pursuits?
The moment is here *now*,
for me to turn around
and surrender my life
to almighty God.
Your grace, Dear God,
clears away all obstacles in my path,
and illuminates my soul.
I return back
to my divine home
in this special land
beyond life and death.

One who is sluggish
remains stuck in the marshes of time,
and never returns.
No, I will not belong to the sluggish,
for my love of life
and my love for you, God,
is vast and intense.
This love is the light
that illuminates my path,
and sweeps out all the sluggishness
from my being.
In order to *love* life and God,
no special striving is necessary.
Through vigilant observing
and subtle listening into life,
God's magnificence reveals itself
in the little things of everyday life.

The divine light shines everywhere,
eternally and always.
Of what use is it
that I read
about the divine light?
Of what use is it to speak
about the divine light?
Absolulutely no use at all,
if I am not truly ready
to surrender my life
to You, the Light of All Lights.
Therefore, I now
merge seamlessly and silently
with Your divine light.

*S*erene and lucid now,
the Light of All Lights
has easily
found my heart
and transformed me.

61

*I*t may be so,
that the body is ill beyond cure,
or disabled.
I do not doubt,
and I allow my thoughts no opportunity
to roam in dark abysses.
I raise myself above
my shadows and my weaknesses *now*,
and align myself
with my inner strengths.

Yes, they are all within me,
those divine powers
which You, God, have granted.
Without hesitation, I accept
these illustrious gifts,
and dedicate myself completely
to You, the giver.

My innermost being,
my radiant soul
was never afflicted
with illness or disability –
this I see clearly,
of this I am certain.

I set the whole of my attention
on the divine source,
which pours forth
from deep within my heart.
After my physical death,
I will return
to this source,
but in fact, I already live
from this magnificent source *now*,
and am pervaded and nourished
by its sacred water.

Wrong understanding
led me to wrong actions.
Because my heart has become clear,
and is now dedicated to God,
I sense remorse.
Remorse means insight.
Insight shows me
that my mistakes once recognized
will not be repeated.
This ending induces liberation
from wrong actions.
Every good intention
is supported and accompanied
by the divine flow of grace.
Therefore, I entrust
my life to You, oh God.

63

I can see
that each breath
is a sacred gift,
and each thought
a sacred power.
My essential being
is truly a divine gift.
Without hesitation
and without doubt,
I accept
this superb divine gift
completely and unconditionally.

Never again will I look away,
never again will I
place all my ego-centered attention
on my own life.
When I look away,
I see nothing,
and when I see nothing,
my life is dull and pitiable.
No, I look out
and see the world
with the eyes of love.
I see my fellow human beings
with gentle eyes.
Yes, I look out,
for the world and human beings
are *not* irrelevant to me.

Light of All Lights,
You permeate and illuminate
all living beings.
Bless, heal, and bestow liberation
to all readers
now and through all eternity.

From heart to heart

- Master M -

Mario Mantese

If you would like to attend a gathering
with Master M
or if you have any other questions,
please contact Mark Albin at
organization@mariomantese.com
or refer to the website at
www.mariomantese.com

You Are the World

This inspired series of aphorisms is a poetic revelation of the philosophical and spiritual depths of Master M.

ISBN: 978-3-7431-0454-9
Publisher: www.bod.de/www.bod.ch

In Touch with a Universal Master

This unusual biography portrays the life and boundless spiritual workings of Master M through narratives of his very early students.

ISBN: 978-3-7431-8313-1
Publisher: www.bod.de/www.bod.ch

The Art of Not Being

In this profound and concise work Mario Mantese (Master M) directs his focus to the art of seeing as an awakening being, one living in the world, but not attached to the world.

ISBN: 978-3-7412-3432-3
Publisher: www.bod.de/www.bod.ch

Blessings – A Man of Miracles

This collection of twenty-one narratives from people who have known Mario Mantese – Master M – for many years, is a fascinating and insightful view into the life and work of a modern spiritual master. Over 200 of his clear, straightforward, and often humorous responses to spiritual and philosophical questions are included.

ISBN: 978-3-7386-8059-1
Publisher: www.bod.de/www.bod.ch

In the Heart of the World

This very personal autobiography offers a detailed and luminous description of Master M's journey to the core of the universe, and allows the reader to fathom the path of cosmic mastery.

ISBN: 978-3-7386-7267-1
Publisher: www.bod.de/www.bod.ch

What You Really Are

Master M responds in 18 very clear and vibrant chapters to the deepest spiritual and philosophical questions of our time.

ISBN: 978-3-7322-0193-8
Publisher: www.bod.de/www.bod.ch

In the Land of Silence

This autobiographical novel depicts a seeker's fateful encounter with a spiritual master in the Himalayas; from his challenging initiation to his deep realization.

ISBN: 978-3-8423-9166-6
Publisher: www.bod.de/www.bod.ch

The Taoist – The Secret Life

The story of a sincere young woman in search of truth encountering an authentic Toaist master in the forest. A novel of devotion and ancient wisdom set in China

ISBN 978-3-7528-7867-7
Publisher: www.bod.de/www.bod.ch

.